T0196971

I Remembered
I am Eternally Divine

TRAVIS 'NATURAL' HUNTLEY

BALBOA
PRESS

A DIVISION OF HAY HOUSE

Balboa Press books may be ordered through booksellers or by contacting:

Balboa Press
A Division of Hay House
1663 Liberty Drive
Bloomington, IN 47403
www.balboapress.com
1 (877) 407-4847

Print information available on the last page.

ISBN: 978-1-5043-7183-4 (sc)
ISBN: 978-1-5043-7182-7 (hc)
ISBN: 978-1-5043-7184-1 (e)

Library of Congress Control Number: 2016920909

Balboa Press rev. date: 02/07/2017

Contents

Preface

A Gathering Of The Tribe
By Author of The More Beautiful World our Hearts Know is Possible
Charles Eisenstein

"Once upon a time a great tribe of people lived in a world far away from ours. Whether far away in space, or in time, or even outside of time, we do not know. They lived in a state of enchantment and joy that few of us today dare to believe could exist, except in those exceptional peak experiences when we glimpse the true potential of life and mind. One day the shaman of the tribe called a meeting. They gathered around him, and he spoke very solemnly. "My friends," he said, "there is a world that needs our help. It is called earth, and its fate hangs in the balance. Its humans have reached a critical point in their collective birthing, and they will be stillborn without our help. Who would like to volunteer for a mission to this time and place, and render service to humanity?" "Tell us more about his mission," they asked. "I am glad you asked, because it is no small thing. I will put you into a deep, deep trance, so complete that you will forget who you are. You will live a human life, and in the beginning you will completely forget your origins. You will forget even our language and your own true name. You will be separated from the wonder and beauty of our world, and from the love that bathes us all. You will miss it deeply, yet you will not know what it is you are missing. You will only remember the love and beauty that we know to be normal as a longing in your heart. Your memory will take the form of an intuitive knowledge, as you plunge into the painfully marred earth, that a more beautiful world is possible. "As you grow up in that world, your knowledge will be under constant assault. You will be told in a million ways that a world of destruction, violence, drudgery, anxiety, and degradation is normal. You may go through a time when you are completely alone, with no allies to affirm your knowledge of a more beautiful world. You may plunge into a depth of despair that we, in our world of light, cannot imagine. But no matter what, a spark of knowledge will never leave you. A memory of your true origin will be encoded in your DNA. That spark will lie within you, inextinguishable, until one day it is awakened. "You see, even though you will feel, for a time, utterly alone, you will not be alone. I will send you assistance, help that you will experience as miraculous, experiences that you will describe as transcendent. For a few moments or hours or

TRAVIS 'NATURAL' HUNTLEY

days, you will reawaken to the beauty and the joy that is meant to be. You will see it on earth, for even though the planet and its people are deeply wounded, there is beauty there still, projected from past and future onto the present as a promise of what is possible and a reminder of what is real. "You will also receive help from each other. As you begin to awaken to your mission you will meet others of our tribe. You will recognize them by your common purpose, values, and intuitions, and by the similarity of the paths you have walked. As the condition of the planet earth reaches crisis proportions, your paths will cross more and more. The time of loneliness, the time of thinking you might be crazy, will be over. "You will find the people of your tribe all over the earth, and become aware of them through the long-distance communication technologies used on that planet. But the real shift, the real quickening, will happen in face-to-face gatherings in special places on earth. When many of you gather together you will launch a new stage on your journey, a journey which, I assure you, will end where it began. Then, the mission that lay unconscious within you will flower into consciousness. Your intuitive rebellion against the world presented you as normal will become an explicit quest to create a more beautiful one. "In the time of loneliness, you will always be seeking to reassure yourself that you are not crazy. You will do that by telling people all about what is wrong with the world, and you will feel a sense of betrayal when they don't listen to you. You will be hungry for stories of wrongness, atrocity, and ecological destruction, all of which confirm the validity of your intuition that a more beautiful world exists. But after you have fully received the help I will send you, and the quickening of your gatherings, you will no longer need to do that. Because, you will Know. Your energy will thereafter turn toward actively creating that more beautiful world." A tribeswoman asked the shaman, "How do you know this will work? Are you sure your shamanic powers are great enough to send us on such a journey?" The shaman replied, "I know it will work because I have done it many times before. Many have already been sent to earth, to live human lives, and to lay the groundwork for the mission you will undertake now. I've been practicing! The only difference now is that many of you will venture there at once. What is new in the time you will live in, is that the Gatherings are beginning to happen." A tribesman asked, "Is there a danger we will become lost in that world, and never wake up from the shamanic trance? Is there a danger that the despair, the cynicism, the pain of separation will be so great that it will extinguish the spark of hope, the spark of our true selves and origin, and that we will be separated from our beloved ones forever?" The shaman replied, "That is impossible. The more deeply you get lost, the more powerful the help I will send you. You might experience it at the time as a collapse of your personal world, the loss of everything important to you. Later you will recognize the gift within it. We will never abandon you." Another man

TRAVIS 'NATURAL' HUNTLEY

asked, "Is it possible that our mission will fail, and that this planet, earth, will perish?" The shaman replied, "I will answer your question with a paradox. It is impossible that your mission will fail. Yet, its success hangs on your own actions. The fate of the world is in your hands. The key to this paradox lies within you, in the feeling you carry that each of your actions, even your personal, secret struggles within, has cosmic significance. You will know then, as you do now, that everything you do matters. God sees everything." There were no more questions. The volunteers gathered in a circle, and the shaman went to each one. The last thing each was aware of was the shaman blowing smoke in his face. They entered a deep trance and dreamed themselves into the world where we find ourselves today."

Foreword

There is a beauty in existence that will always remain evident no matter what story we tell, what point of view we are in, or how we decide to play the game. That beauty lives in the heart of creative expression. The one driving force inherent in all life is the unyielding capacity to create and express. The entire universe is a reflection of that truth. The governing function in our true state of being, as spirit, is the desire to inexhaustibly explore and apply our unlimited creative potential. That sets the stage for the most miraculous occurrence based on our choice and our willingness to do so. This immediate understanding brings us to the choice we have all made to exist right now in the story of human beings on earth, the story of our galaxy, and the story of our participatory universe.

The most amazing thing about life is that it only wants to move forward. It only wants to experience more of itself, explore more of itself, express more of itself. So when it comes to being Source Creators, created in the same likeness as the source of all existence, we have the same inspiration and resiliency to do the same. After thousands of years of telling the same story of fear and limitation in so many different ways, we have finally hit our threshold and realized it's time to tell a different story. This awakening has sparked a beautiful burning desire in so many around the world to not only witness change, but to assume the responsibility to be it themselves. Truth be told that is the only way change will arrive, and even more so, thrive and sustain. So many brilliant minds and radiant souls across the globe are conjuring up new approaches to this human experience while accessing grand wisdom that has always been available since before time was a necessary component of the learning process. It is those of us choosing to be on the leading edge of driving this story to new frontiers of our creative potential that are acting as the guiding light revealing just what can be possible when we decide to see it done; simply because we can.

As more continue to awaken and live in this new awareness of self, ever expanding to encompass all things, more begin to connect with each other building not just the individual aspect of creating change, but the communal. The more the collective consciousness builds in such regard, the more it becomes a way of life. The more it becomes a way of life, the more the idea has catapulted into critical mass and consequentially the point of no return. This understanding in association with the necessity of building a support system, in greater unification, led to the creation of The Light Beings Community, where we have birthed a practice dedicated to the idea of living in uncompromising truth. As the community grew we learned two very important lessons. One, that this is something many have been seeking, and two, we were not alone. Witnessing the way these communities are rising and developing has provided an irrefutable confirmation that we all are feeling the desire and necessity to not only thrust forward in our creative potential, but to learn how to do it from unconditional love. It is the love in us that has sparked the desire to change the story. It is the love in us that has brought a greater awareness out of compassion. It is the love in us that has revealed our connection to all things in existence. The more I come across such radiant souls like Travis Huntley, the truer it becomes, and the more grateful I feel. Which only compels myself and others to persist. The honor to be of service is the willingness to expand from love. What we shall create from there, is the story of a civilization more aligned with its sense of self, its inherent nature, and its unlimited creative potential.

Here's to changing the course of history. Here's to changing what it means to have the human experience. Here's to finally realizing on a global scale that we truly are all in this together.

My Honor, My Gratitude, My Love,

Kevin Walton
Founder of The Light Beings Community

"A message for thee
for all to see
in love we shall be
abundant and free"

Jessenia Cardoso

Introduction

The words presented in the pages to come were written in Jamaica, Peru and the United States over the past few years. The words read in this book are words from spirit within, I recommend reading these words with an open heart and mind without judgment. I'm simply now sharing words that my intuition guided me to bring forth to the public. I now invite everyone who reads this book to take action by sharing with your friends and family whatever you feel will empower and uplift them.

I now choose to allow the vibration of my essence to resonate at the highest levels of joy, love, compassion and celebration. Remembering to live in this now moment; choosing to no longer live in a state of worry, fear or anxiety of what may happen next. Instead, I choose to focus on contributing my energy, talents and gifts here now with intention to be of service to humanity however I am intuitively guided to do so.

I am now grounding the divine will of source here on Earth as I continue to have the courage to emit love unconditionally. As a force of love individualized with unique gifts to give and roles to play, I am creating a new story, a world in harmony with everything in all time and space. As I continue to become self-realized, aware of my nature underneath the skin, I begin to see myself in my neighbor and realize I am one; I am interconnected in this realm and beyond. Realizing I am inseparable, I finally see that I am GOD, Source, consciousness, spirit 'whatever label I wish to place on it' individualized expressing itself in various forms.

My natural state of being is a state of bliss and my source of love is within. Remembering this knowledge and wisdom my ancestors obtained and preserved prior to my existence then integrating the new profound scientific research and technologies of today. Reminding those who may have forgot heaven is already here waiting for us to recognize it and choose to live it.

Choosing to love in the most challenging situations is the key to the gates of the kingdom of heaven. I am now given experiences to learn from, to see if I am capable of sustaining a reality in harmony with the innate loving frequencies of Mother Earth. I get to choose a reality being fed to me through the tell-lie-vision and movies consistently promoting fear, materialism, violence, division and self-hate; or I can choose a reality of love, the choice is mine.

I now have the opportunity to refuse to give anyone or anything who enters into my reality the power and control over my state of being. I can choose to react with anger, fear, hatred or frustration; or I can choose to respond with love and gratitude for being my greatest teachers and mirror reflections of my self showing up to remind me to love and accept what ever is arising.

All of my experiences are given to me for the contribution and expansion of the collective, due to the interconnected nature of all life. Each moment has prepared me for my role and purpose of existing on Earth. The power of my being is limitless now that I returned to my natural state of being beyond the restrictions, filters and barriers I adopted from my parents, school, society, religion and culture. I choose now to no longer be my own skeptic and critic. I choose to go beyond the mind's constant chatter, transmutable by believing and trusting myself, going beyond all doubt. Getting out of my own way with confidence and faith, knowing everything is in divine order, then utilizing my boundless divine gifts and attributes to create a global community with love, cooperation and compassion as its pillars.

I choose now to release anything that is no longer serving me to allow the expansion of the vibration I am emanating. I choose now to release any habits and desires that are no longer in alignment with the reality I would like to create in this present moment. My reality mirrors my beliefs, and the vibration I am resonating at is the mirror of the experience I will ultimately align with. Creating a new reality showing up in the form of manifestation or what some may call miracles appearing in my reality.

I chose to align with a partner of integrity, self-respect, self-love, while living a purpose driven lifestyle, by possessing those same attributes myself. When I truly began to love myself, I was no longer willing to harm myself spiritually or physically. I chose to partake in activities that are serving my energetic frequency, my physical body increases with no limit on how much it can expand, unlocking my physical body's greatest potential.

I chose to believe in the illusion that I am somehow disconnected from Source and separate from one another; which may have caused me to to lose faith and belief in myself, creating a mind state of dependency. I forgot that the omnipresence, the omnipotence and the omniscient divine wisdom has been within me the whole time. This is why all of the ancient teachers, sages and masters from all over the globe expressed the importance to meditate and listen to the voice within. The true guru is Source within. Now that I know I have the omnipotent power within me to transform any circumstance in my current reality, I choose to express love to all with no limitations or judgments. I now choose to focus on living my life aware of my abundance over worry in an illusory state of lack.

I now see my life is about sharing my voice to add value to others. I realize my life is about much more than the accumulation of the energetic tool some refer to as money or legal tender; which has no gold or silver backing. I realized the only value it has is the value I put on it and the more value I put out the more money comes in. I can now choose to use my money to serve my purpose in balance with my desire to enjoy life or to serve money for my own selfish desires, materialism, greed, power and vanity.

I am now witness to many serendipitous events and gatherings as I focus my intention on Source's will and my heart is in a state of unconditional joy, peace, love, harmony, and happiness. I now recognize no matter what I experience in life, it is here to serve me. When I began to choose to be of service to all life, Source then began to be of service to me in monumental ways. I am now choosing to live a way of life driven by unconditional love my children and grandchildren will thank me for later.

Abundance

The Earth is full of abundance of all kinds
I opened my eyes to see the abundance Mother Earth
provides
the sun, the rain and the lay lines
an abundance of energy traveling through my spine

Mother provide me with everything I will ever need
why do so many of us choose to be a slave instead of
living free
when we live of the land, there's no need for money
the only thing I need is my hands to build and grow what
I eat

I return back to nature to live not just for a summer retreat
I remain there and walk in my bare feet
I sing loud and free
allowing GOD to be the voice of my speech
giving words of wisdom to all whom I meet

I listen to the birds, the wind and the sounds of the rain
I listen close and choose to turn off the sounds of pain
I live free in peace, authentically never ashamed
I return to nature to reclaim
the abundance provided amongst this earthly plain

I am free to stay and remain in nature for the rest of my
days
living with the highest form of energy in every way
being as a child I begin to play
I wake up early to the light of the sun's rays
choosing to meditate and pray
giving thanks to have an opportunity to live in another way

Babylon's Kryptonite

I give thanks to be here upon Mother Earth
I now know why I was put here for birth
to become self-realized and aware I am the true church
it's a shame most don't realize it until our bodies are in a hearse

Then I might have to come back down for another rebirth
because I believed I am just the body now fertilizing the dirt
I choose to become self realized first
to assure my return to Source after my time served

Before I got caught up into distractions and infatuations
so I could focus on my life purpose and passions
not what's the latest fashions
I spent time meditating and fasting giving up sensory satisfaction

To become aware of my whole self not just a ration
I am perfect whole and complete not just a fraction
sent to Earth to learn from my experiences and lessons
life began when I to ask life's most important questions

Why am I here? What happens when I die?
all my answers were found inside
when I meditated and became GOD realized
aware of my true self, able to read in between the lines
and see the lies

I can live the rest of my life and completely deny
or I can face the facts and begin to fly
my ancestors built pyramids so they could rise their
vibration so high
they would leave their bodies then astral project through
the sky

Through the cosmos faster than the speed of light
to the infinite web of love no sign of fright
I close my eyes and choose to meditate tonight
going inside to remember my own insight

I am love
I chose to give my love to everyone in sight
I no longer feed Babylon the energy it thrives on, which
is fright
love and light is Babylon's kryptonite

GOD

GOD is love

GOD is below and above

GOD is the essence that can rise never fall

GOD is all creatures that crawl

GOD is nature, the sounds of the birds and water falls

GOD is the bark on the trees

GOD is the veins in all leaves

GOD is the water that flows down the streams

GOD is the soil which the plants need

GOD is the blood that flows from my brain to the toes on my feet

GOD is all plants and fruits we reap

GOD is all animals, those that fly and creep

GOD is in my dreams when I sleep

GOD is the lessons and circumstances manifested into reality

GOD is all regardless of the technicality

GOD is divine bliss and tranquility

GOD is everywhere as far as the eye can see

GOD is even in the dimensions that aren't usually seen

GOD is in the words I speak
GOD is pure love with no flaws indeed
GOD is everything in existence
GOD is spirit
GOD is I

Gratitude

I give thanks to GOD almighty
living inside of me
I give thanks to GOD almighty
living inside the grass and seas

I give thanks to GOD almighty
I give thanks for the people being gravitated towards me
I give thanks to GOD almighty
I give thanks to now have the courage to live free

I give thanks to GOD almighty
I give thanks to have friends with eyes whom can see
I give thanks to GOD almighty
I give thanks for friends who are no longer afraid to just be

I give thanks to GOD almighty
I give thanks to have the ability to conceive
I give thanks to GOD almighty
I give thanks to be able to sit down, relax and read

I give thanks to GOD almighty
I give thanks to know how to perceive so it's impossible
to be deceived
I give thanks to GOD almighty
I give thanks to have been given these words to give freely

I give thanks to GOD almighty
I give thanks to have time to meditate then foresee
I give thanks to GOD almighty
I give thanks to mother earth for giving birth to a new creed
to plant seeds of wisdom into the minds and hearts of all
as far as eyes can see

I give thanks to GOD almighty
I give thanks to those planting veggies and fruit trees
so future generations will have all the food they'll ever need
I give thanks to GOD almighty

Higher purpose

What is the meaning of a higher purpose
it means I sit and meditate to allow my role to surface
listen then allow my third eye to open like a lotus
vibrating when I choose to focus

Who am I serving? My physical senses of the body
or the essence of all some may call GOD almighty
my eternal divine self or the tool known as the psyche
be sure to meditate in the morning and nightly
so I may increase my frequency even if it's just slightly

My purpose was chosen before I arrived to Earth
way before I was birthed
I was called for a mission first
love is what quenches my soul's thirst
I choose to share love even if it hurts

I give love to everyone who enters into my reality
I choose to remove my dogmatic mentality
and replace it with spiritually
this improves my vitality
then creates a personality
that chooses to live in tranquility

Over stress, suffering and self-sabotaging
occurring when I am living selfishly
until I remember to live selflessly
then GOD served me ultimately

As long as I live purposefully
aware my true self lives eternally for eternity
never to return to Earth again certainly
because the mission is complete permanently

I am Divine Infinite Love

Love is innate in all beings
but for most seeing is believing
so I lived my life trying to achieve
love from an outside source because I'd been deceived

And know longer believed
love could possibly reside inside all including me
but this is far far far from truth indeed
because love is formless and unseen

Residing beneath the material form I see
its up to me to realize love is an inherited gift given free
and could never be bought with any amount of money
so why is it I tried to please others and seek approval shamefully

While my spirit awaits patiently
to meditate then learn how to just be
to love all of my natural self and recognize my beauty
then awaken and realize I am one with GOD almighty
I am a co worker to the divine plan indeed

TRAVIS 'NATURAL' HUNTLEY

To bring peace, love and unity
to all in every country
I asked myself the question, what would I do for free
how could I utilize my talents to serve while living with dignity
fulfilling my life's purpose is true integrity

Knowing my spirit lives infinitely
and is connected to all in all of the universes even the grass
and the trees
so please don't rely on me
or depend on anyone but yourself for answers
because you were born with everything you will ever need

I am One

I am one with everyone I do and don't know
I am the essence of all in all of the cosmos
I am spirit, when I know thyself I grow
I am my highest self and the low
loving both as equal is when I began to glow

I am love incarnated into flesh called the human form
I am a unique piece of the puzzle, so there's no need to
be the norm
so many of us trying to be the same the puzzle is now deformed
now is the time to become informed
of our divine unique presence awaiting to perform

I am nature, the forest, the garden and the crops
I am the water that flows from the mountain tops
I am the wind that blows and never stops
I am everything that exist, the soil, the crystals and the rocks

I am the grass, the trees and the seas
I am everything I can think of in my wildest dreams
I am star dust in this realm for all eyes to see
I am everything, nothing and all that will ever be

GOD is everywhere including in all humans that is
mathematically placed
I am matter and space
I am spirit embodied not the religion, class gender or race
I am perfect whole and complete and could never be replaced
I am a unique expression of GOD whom has descended
to earth and now has a face

Know Thyself

Why was I born into this human form
to be myself or try to fit in and be like the norm
to be the flower or the thorn
to live free or conform

When I realized I am more than the physical I was reborn
now awakened to my true self, infinite, pure love, living in
bliss over morn
why is it I felt separated and torn
I forgot I am everything and in the company of all we'll
ever need and more

Always in battle with others unaware of my oneness with
all from shore to shore
Caucasians, Asians, Africans whom they referred to as Moors
why fight when I was sent to earth to assist and restore
reminding all of our inherited peace and love at birth
utilizing positive metaphors

I grow what I eat instead of relying on the stores
living self sustained of the land so I pray It pours
while raising the love vibration up from the floor
by traveling the world as if I was on tour

Sharing love with all, the rich and the so called poor
encouraging every actor, athlete and artist to support
to unite everyone from shore to shore
know thyself
need I say more

Love

Love is the essence and vibration of all things
Love is the force that resides inside and is the yin to my yang
Love is priceless and can't be bought or sold only exchanged
Love is inside to remind me we're all the same

Love is the invisible net that connects all in existence
Love cannot be separated by any man made fence
Love is GOD and I am GOD sent
Love never judges and only knows thankfulness

Love is Mother Earth and all of her nature
Love is the trees that provide me with oxygen and paper
Love is the fruits, vegetables and spices given to me for flavor
Love is the weapon of choice, no need for knives, guns or razors

Love is the highest state ever achieved
Love is the ultimate gift given or received
Love is timeless so I removed my watch and choose to live free
Love is the only force I have so I use it infinitely

Love is the common denominator and the factor
Love is the guru and the master
Love is the essence that binds us all together like plaster
Love is the essence I seemed to run after

Love is inside of all even dark matter
Love is the source behind all, even the world's disasters
Love is the voice I hear inside once I removed my minds chatter
Love is the prerequisite to enter heaven on earth some may
call the rapture

Mother Earth

The sweet essence of nature's breeze
as the wind passes over and through the leaves
allowing all of humanity to breath
I chose to give more thanks to the oxygen I get from trees
and the smell of the flower's aroma that attracts the birds
and the bees

The harmonious sounds of crickets singing at night
when the sun is tired and no longer able to share her light
the crickets are awakening to share their delight
the musical symphony of Mother Earth blesses all even
those with no sight
the sounds of Mother Earth who soothes my ears while
watching the moonlight

The amazing taste of a mango right after it drops to earth's floor
mother provides everything I request and more
I return to nature where there's no store
giving thanks to mother's living room, I enter freely there's
no door

TRAVIS 'NATURAL' HUNTLEY

I look around and find springs, rivers and streams
mother's rivers here to wash my clothes, dishes, hands and feet
no bathtubs and sinks
springs to provide me with all the water to drink
while mother's streams give me sounds of waterfalls to no
longer think

I Give thanks to the sounds of the crickets and birds that
will forever sing
to the wind that will blow to assure we will forever breathe
to the fruits of the trees we will forever reap
to the water forever flowing providing us with nourishment
for all to drink

Namaste

The essence within me is the same essence within all
coming to this realization, the walls that separate us begin
to fall
everyone loving everyone, even their so called flaws
whether I'm short, tall, big, or small
born in summer, spring, winter or fall

All it took was a simple remembrance of who I really am
the essence in me is the same essence in the Earth, moon,
and the stars
including the beings that may reside in places like Jupiter
and Mars
I open my heart to all near and far
knowing all is one and I am the driver and the car

I remembered my body gets thrown away when Source is
all done
no longer choosing Earth to express, remember and have fun
spirit then returns back to the same essence as everyone
everything in existence even the sun

When death is near there's nothing to fear
I prepare to leave by meditating upon why I've come here
share our pure love and light to all whom can be seen on
this sphere
I keep my heart open and all my chakras clear
and my body pure, so I ingest in the foods that Mother
Earth provides here

I've become aware of what it takes to open my third eye
this knowledge has been hidden so I educated myself to
know why
to elevate my frequency so high the sky can no longer deny
my ability to do anything including fly
I was born to speak, love and remember to shine
I vow to be bold, expressive and at peace while among the lies

Open The Eyes of the Blind

I take time to relax
away from distractions and daily ESPN stats
I remember to go inside where there is never lack
I am full of abundance of an abundance of light awaiting
for me to tap

When I listen to the voice inside
things begin to manifest here on the outside
I begin to realize I am GOD in disguise
individualized on this Earth to express and ask why

Why am I here
for a purpose to unite everyone near
I took a glimpse into my higher self and stood clear
allowing GOD inside to come forth and impact everyone near
finally realizing I am an expression of GOD whom has
appeared

For real
I may choose to appeal
because what I hear may sound surreal
I then open my mind and listen from the heart then believe
what I feel

Remember

What am I here to do
I am here to speak the truth
I go inside to the true school
I listen to the voice and relearn the rules
how to utilize my own GOD given tools
then remember I am a unique droplet in the same pool

Remember I am one and I choose to live in unison
with less friction so there's no need for police and politician
I chose love as my religion
uniting all Muslims, Jews, Buddhist, Hindus, and Christian
African, Asian, Hispanic and Caucasian

All united as one
I am not quitting until the job is done
until we are all living together having fun
all utilizing our skills and talents for one mission
to live in a new position
were there's no more competition

Peace, love and unity is the message and the vision
I chose to turn off the tel lie vision
to then tune inside myself and begin to listen
I heard I am GOD in the flesh that has now risen
whether I am Muslim, Jew, Buddhist, Hindu or Christian

Remind

I remind myself to speak with precision
free from the delusion of separation and division
seeing unity in my vision
love is the message and the mission

I remind myself I am one and can never be separated
and could never dream of being segregated
I keep my heart open so my frequency is elevated
I choose to live everyday celebrated

I remind myself why I've come here
to raise the love vibration and have the courage to go
beyond all fear
and share my love with all to who may come near
to rise the frequency of this earthly sphere

I remind myself to freely express myself
without the need for approval from someone else
expressing fully to assure all hearts are felt
until love is the common expression I see nothing else

I remind the myself of my greatness and the importance
to believe
I can do anything now that I know I've been deceived
into believing I am only this body that gets thrown away
when my
divine eternal spirit is ready to leave
then return back to source after waiting so patiently

I remind myself to return to nature and live of the land
no longer depending on the man they call uncle sam
now is the when I choose to stand
for every women child and man

I remind myself to listen to the songs from the birds
the voice of the trees that may at first sound absurd
truth is the only component of their words that can be
heard
I allow my ears to be marinated by nature's voice begging
to be conserved
and to return so I may relearn my soul's true concern

Take This Time

Take this time to know thyself
Take this time to breath
Take this time to express thyself
Take this time to be free
Take this time to be thyself
Take this time to lead
Take this time to expand thyself
Take this time to see
Take this time to love thyself
Take this time to feel
Take this time to go inside thyself
Take this time to be seen
Take this time to find thyself
Take this time to grow
Take this time to reveal thyself
Take this time to know
Take this time to believe in thyself
Take this time to share

Take this time to have faith in thyself
Take this time to trust
Take this time to cleanse thyself
Take this time to be
Take this time to share love with all from sea to sea

Transformation

It's time to show the youth how it's supposed to be done
take them back to when hip hop use to be positive
expression and fun
when I walked, there was no need for guns
the only ammo I need is my tongue and my lungs

Life began when I opened my mind
when I was no longer confined to this thing called time
then I began to see in between the lines
keeping my heart wide open able to share the divine

Eyes wide open now able to share my light that has been
hidden in disguise
now aware that GOD lives inside and not somewhere in
the sky
it is up to me to realize
I've been hypnotized into believing lies
then I woke up and chose to rise

Or I can choose to deny
my abundance that enables me to fly
and begin to live beyond fear on the front line
expressing lyrical potency through ears and down the spine
written with words that just so happen to rhyme

In no time
no space only divine
with pure light to shine
into the obis of darkness awaiting to refine

Unconditional Happiness

I choose to remain Happy amongst all cost
remain at peace even when I experience material loss
allow my heart to stay open even if I may come off as soft
show the physical body, Source is the boss

So the flow of my spirit continues to grow
the flow stops when my heart is closed
when the illusion of fear enters my consciousness, the flow
stops as if it were froze
which is why I decide to love and accept like a pro

Refrain from defending myself when there's no true threat
choosing to respond rather than react as if there's a knife
at my neck
there's no weapon at all maybe just a lack of respect
or a point of view different from my own mind set

I remain humble and open my mindset
before I do things I may forever regret
or forget my true self is much more than flesh
I am the essence I leave Mother Earth with when I've
finished all my test

All my circumstances are test to see if I can do my best
to love regardless of what happens next
vowing from this day forward to live the rest of my life
without stress
because my spirit deserves nothing less

My spirit is choosing to express
to do what I love and no longer allow my voice to be repressed
then I came to the point in my life when I asked the
question, what's next?
then I take some time to meditate and reflect

Upon what happens when my body is laid down to rest
I return back to the same dimension as the rest with no flesh
the same space where I dream and astral project
into my original state of peace, love and unconditional happiness

Transmute Reality

As I walk down the street I see reflections or what I may call mirrors
I look deep into their eyes then realized they're myself whom has appeared
disguised as flesh, full of love, no room for fear
or what some may call false evidence appearing real
to teach me lessons and remind me why I've come here

I see my purpose now so vivid and clear
here on a mission to unite everyone near
my dreams begin to appear as if they were actually real
a class full of lessons from another dimensional field

I choose to unite and realize we're all in this together
you, me, the elements, GOD and the weather
I've lived of the land with mother nature the best teacher ever
beyond fear fully aware my spirit lives on forever

Aware time is not linear and my body is 99% space
I am an infinite being here to transmute into my original state
aware I am perfect, whole and complete regardless of my race
or how much money I am able to accumulate

It only takes a simple remembrance of myself to take place
to transmute my current place of residents, resonance and fate
at a rate and pace everyone could then replicate
then celebrate my arrival into an expanded state utilizing
my body as a star gate

Now aware I am source in the flesh vibrating at three
dimensional pace
I remembered my reality is determined by my inner
energetic rate
I create my reality and it is I who has chooses my
circumstantial state
choosing to have faith that I have what it takes
for GOD'S sake

Faith is believing in myself
remembering I am source is true wealth
that has been hidden in stealth
deep within self is where it can be seen and felt

Life is like poker, the cards dealt can be changed
when my love is rearranged into myself again
it's so simple and plain
and so easy to obtain
when I stay in my lane
away from toxins and pain
disciplined enough to only allow peace and love to flow
through my veins
in order to reclaim my purpose upon this earthly plane
once again

A purpose for all of whom awakes this way
and chooses to apply our skills each day
to serve and love all, constantly giving thanks
while taking time to go inside ourselves to meditate and
pray

So I can listen to the voice inside intending to say
do what I love and don't go astray
be as children and take time to play
to see heaven on Earth with no delay

Vision

I see I am awakening
I see since I am awake
I see I am living free and independent
I see since I am free and independent

I see I must grow my own food to be self-sustained
I see since I am self-sustained living with nature
I see I am free from dependency on the system
I see since I am no longer in dependency

I see if the system were to crumble I will survive
I see since I am alive
I see I am coming to complete knowledge of self and the
power of love
I see since I know thyself and the power of love

I see love invading the consciousness of all
I see since love is in all
I see love in everyone
I see since I witness love in everyone

I see I will know longer fear people anymore
I see since I fear no more
I see there is no more war
I see since I see no war

I see peace in the world
I see since I brought peace to the world
I see I am stewarding the world
I see since I am stewarding the world

I see am I learning that nature provides everything
I see since I realized nature provides everything
I see I removed myself from my chains
I see since I am no longer chained

I see I am no longer enslaved
I see since I am no longer a slave
I see I am now in a selfless state
I see since I am now in a selfless state

I see I am choosing to making a difference
I see since I am now making a difference
I see I am serving all
I see since I am now serving all

I am doing whatever it takes to share love with the world
I see since I am sharing love
I see I am choosing to be thy brother's keeper

Voice Box of GOD

I enjoy nature and the smell of the rain falling
giving nourishment to the soil where the worms and snakes
are usually crawling
I return to nature to remember my calling
to plant seeds of wisdom and love like bee's an pollen

I travel back and forth to Earth to share love with all creeds
reminding billions of beings love is the force that
transmutes our genes
then able to beam pure light into all even those whom
cant be seen
I am a warrior of light, I birth upon Earth until my
mission is complete

Until all on Earth are loving their neighbors
realizing we're all born each others saviors
so why did I spend my life trying to get to the majors
causing me to forget I've come to give favors
without expecting any fruits for my labors

In order to complete the mission I must know how
tapping into the omniscience of GOD,
I remembered time is not linear and there is only now
realizing I am GOD here to share love in every way I
know how
in each and every moment of now

All knowledge and wisdom is available, all I must do is
seek and it shall be found
GOD is living inside awaiting to use my voice to speak, I
just listen for the sound
meditating allows me to hear the voice of GOD
encouraging me to speak loud
the words spoken are all of ours
so there's know need to be proud

Warrior of Light

Oh ancestors in the unseen realm
I thank you for loving me on this day here and now
while I give the people inspirational gifts through my voice
mixed with sounds
unloading lyrical rounds instilled with vibrations that
uplift whole towns
encouraging all to become self realized this time around

Giving love and light over fear
living life to the fullest utilizing love to unite everyone near
giving truth in the form of lyrical spears
that pierces through hearts and speaks to ears
speaking loud and clear
so all have the opportunity to hear

Traveling the whole sphere
opening the hearts and minds of all while encouraging the
people to go beyond fear
and to love instead of expressing hate into the atmosphere
because what I express becomes real
I relax and take time to meditate upon why I've have come
here

Maintaining my peace is success that's for real
being at peace even when death is near
because death is nothing to fear
death is only the beginning of life in another dimensional
sphere

Take a moment to go inside to hear
the voice of GOD that is not heard with ears
patiently awaiting to be heard then expressed to everyone near
I speak what I hear
especially to the ones I hold dear

GOD, peace and love are the common denominators we
all share
I am a warrior of light here to declare
I am GOD individualized now realized so system beware

Closing

I now see everyone across the globe is beginning to realize our apathy and conformity. I now see people realizing we all have families who live in this society and the importance to eliminate our conformity and apathetic ways of life and take action, making a difference now. I now see everyone having enough courage to apply our various unique talents, skills and resources to a common cause for the greater good and most importantly for the future of the youth. I now see everyone unified together choosing to love each other unconditionally. I now see people choosing to travel the globe, country to country, state to state, city to city, walking the streets assisting, inspiring, and motivating people from all walks of life. I now see everyone choosing bliss because bliss is our natural state. I now see people choosing to unify together and hold space for community meditations, potlucks, drum circles, festivals, events, concerts, workshops etc. Joining together as one, collaborating and discussing with one another to discuss solutions we may be able to bring forth in our own communities. I now see people using there voice to add value to those in there families and the community at large. I now see people choosing to give lectures and seminars at high schools, universities, churches, town meetings etc. Now expressing the necessity to remove the inherited social virus of division and separation on all levels; race, class, religion, all of which have been passed down generation to generation. I now see the people choosing to stop all cycles of perpetuating division and putting an end to the cycle by choosing love, acceptance and compassion. I now see people choosing to give solution based information via literature, dvd's, YouTube, radio and media to assist in the process of reminding the people we are all one interconnected web of consciousness. I now see a unified force, assisting and contributing to the following courses of action: Utilize all forms of art to remind the people to love. Expand the frequency of our self which will inevitably increase the frequency of the planet. Remind the people we are all one and interconnected with everything in existence. Remind the people of the equality and oneness of light and dark, yin and yang. Assuring the people remember the dark is our way of reminding our self to share our love and light again. Reminding the people of the infinite divine eternal nature of our spirit to be at peace during our transition. Encourage as many people as we can to do what they love, do what brings us the highest amounts of joy while applying our skills, talents and resources towards making a difference while living a life full of abundance. Remind those who may have forgot to love and have compassion for everyone unconditionally. In doing so we will inevitably lower the crime rate and eliminate war in the streets and throughout the world at large. Encourage our friends and family to meditate, to hear the answers to our questions arriving from within. Remind the people the importance to play, to connect with nature, family and community to restore the human family at large. Encourage the people to live self sustained of the land, to grow what we eat everywhere, fruit trees, home and community gardens to assure humanity thrives. Remind the masses, especially the youth of the importance to respect and steward mother Earth. Even if its simply recycling or picking up litter in our community. Remind the people we can now make a conscious decision to choose from mainstream chemical based products and services or holistic products and services.

Quotes

"In the dawn of physical existence, men knew that death was merely a change of form" "Each of you exists in other realities and other dimensions, and the self that you call yourself is but a small portion of your entire identity""You must learn to listen to the voice of the inner self and work with it. You may also simply ask the inner self to make the answers to problems available on a conscious basis" "We are multidimensional beings who inhabit many realms and who exist throughout eternity; developing continually into more creative and fulfilled individuals" "You create your reality according to your beliefs and expectations, therefore you should examine these carefully. If you do not like some aspect of your world, then examine your own expectations" "You sell yourself short if you believe that you are only a physical organism living within the boundaries cast upon you by time and space. You are a unique individual. You form your physical environment. You are part of all that is. There is no place within you that creativity does not exist" "Your spirit joined itself with flesh, and in flesh, to experience a world of incredible richness, to help create a dimension of reality of colors and of form. Your spirit was born in flesh to enrich a marvelous area of sense awareness, to feel energy made into corporeal form. You are here to use, enjoy, and express yourself through the body." Jane Roberts

"Jesus Christ knew he was God. So wake up and find out eventually who you really are. In our culture, of course, they'll say you're crazy and you're blasphemous, and they'll either put you in jail or in a nut house. However if you wake up in India and tell your friends and relations, 'My goodness, I've just discovered that I'm God,' they'll laugh and say, 'Oh, congratulations, at last you found out." Alan Watts

"The Divine Light is always in man, presenting itself to the senses and to the comprehension, but man rejects it." Giordano Bruno.

"All differences in this world are of degree, and not of kind, because oneness is the secret of everything." Swami Vivekananda

"If I go into the place in myself that is love, and you go into the place in yourself that is love, we are together in love. Then you and I are truly in love, the state of being love. That's the entrance to Oneness. That's the space I entered when I met my guru." Ram Dass

"It's difficult to believe in yourself because the idea of self is an artificial construction. You are, in fact, part of the glorious oneness of the universe. Everything beautiful in the world is within you." Russell Brand

"I believe that Jesus realized his oneness with God and he showed, what he attempted to do was show the way to all of us, how to realize our own oneness with God also, so he's a precursor." Eckhart Tolle

"Quantum physics thus reveals a basic oneness of the universe." Erwin Schrodinger

"The noblest men of all ages, Christian saints of the most transcendent spirituality have attained their wonderful development through the spiritual rays of this planet because of the intense feeling of Oneness with the divine and with all that lives and breathes in the universe." Max Heindel

"The good inside of all of us is wrapped in a layer of apathy, and we forget how much potential we have within us, in each and every one of us, to change the world for the better for ourselves and our children, and thus to bring about oneness." Shari Arison

"Praying without ceasing is not ritualized, nor are there even words. It is a constant state of awareness of oneness with God." Peace Pilgrim

"The God who existed before any religion counts on you to make the oneness of the human family known and celebrated." Desmond Tutu

"We all are so deeply interconnected; we have no option but to love all. Be kind and do good for any one and that will be reflected. The ripples of the kind heart are the highest blessings of the Universe." Amit Ray

"God is not a separate being, God is a state of being and I am a part of that state" Anita Moorjani

"You are immortal; you've existed for billions of years in different manifestations, because you are Life, and Life cannot die. You are in the trees, the butterflies, the fish, the air, the moon, the sun. Wherever you go, you are there, waiting for yourself." Don Miguel Ruiz

"You are one thing only. You are a Divine Being. An all-powerful Creator. You are a Deity in jeans and a t-shirt, and within you dwells the infinite wisdom of the ages and the sacred creative force of All that is, will be and ever was." Anthon St. Maarten

"It is the imagination that argues for the Divine Spark within human beings. It is literally a decent of the World's Soul into all of us." Terrence Mckenna

"I am created in the image of the greatest therefore I am the greatest that ever lived" Master Nigel Henry

"Every man is a divinity in disguise, a god playing the fool.""To the poet, to the philosopher, to the saint, all things are friendly and sacred, all events profitable, all days holy, all men divine." Ralph Waldo Emerson

"There is a divine purpose behind everything - and therefore a divine presence in everything." Neale Donald Walsch

"The divine is not something high above us. It is in heaven, it is in Earth, it is inside us." Morihei Ueshiba

"Man is a universe within himself" Bob Marley

"It's time we realize we are people of Earth. One people, one race" "In every person there is a little child that wants to play...Let them play. The more we let them play the more mature and healthier our spirit is" Wayne William Snellgrove

"Each man is good in the sight of the Great Spirit." Sitting Bull, Teton Sioux

"Faith is a knowledge within the heart, beyond the reach of proof." Kahil Gibran

"These are the vibrations of an angelic being. All their expressions are loving and fair, not shaped or determined by human culture or habit, but by divine harmony and pure will. They may appear to the outsider as doing something personal, but internally their minds are in pure serenity-vast-inscrutable. Who am I describing here? You in your true and natural state." Mooji

"Unified Field Theory in two seconds, Theres a bunch of stuff and its all connected."

We are the universe learning about itself, you are the universe, your not seperate from the universe, you are embeded inside an infinite fractal called the universe and you have a realationship to all those scales all at the same time and the way you do it is not by looking out to try to connect to things, you go in to the center of your existance, to the singularity that holds down your center, the buddhist call this the bindu point, the bindu point is the black whole in the center of your existance." Jaime Janover

"Meditation is not just for relaxation; it's primary purpose is to develop the capacity to respond skillfully and gracefully to life's difficulties as well as its joys." Splashy Tenpin Ricochet

"Love is what we are born with. Fear is what we learn. The spiritual journey is the unlearning of fear and prejudices and the acceptance of love back in our hearts. Love is the essential reality and our purpose on Earth. To be consciously aware of it, to experience love in ourselves and others, is the meaning of life. Meaning does not lie in things. Meaning lies in us." Marianne Williamson

"Love is my religion" "love your enemy" Ziggy Marley

"Love your neighbor as yourself" "Love your enemy" "Above all love one another" "A friend loves at all times" "Whoever does not love does not know God, because God is love" "Over all these virtues put on love, which binds them all together in perfect unity" "Peace comes from within. Do not seek it without." Jesus

"You can search throughout the entire universe for someone who is more deserving of your love and affection than you are yourself, and that person is not to be found anywhere. You, yourself, as much as anybody in the entire universe, deserve your love and affection" "If you truly loved yourself, you could never hurt another." "Teach this triple truth to all: A generous heart, kind speech, and a life of service and compassion are the things which renew humanity." Buddha

"When love awakens in our heart then the selfless service is attained" Radhanath Swami

"Krishna Consciousness spreads wisdom and Knowledge. The main force because of which this movement is spreading is love." Bhakti Charu Swami

"The one who loves all intensely begins perceiving in all living beings a part of himself. He becomes a lover of all, a part and parcel of the Universal Joy. He flows with the stream of happiness, and is enriched by each soul." Yajur Veda

"The human body is the temple of God. One who kindles the light of awareness within gets true light. The sacred flame of your inner shrine is constantly bright. The experience of unity is the fulfillment of human endeavors. The mysteries of life are revealed." Rig Veda

"You will never enter paradise until you have faith and you will not complete your faith until you love one another." Muhammad

"Love glimpsed even for an instant turns the world inside out." "We are born of love; Love is our mother." "Love will find its way through all languages on its own." Rumi

"I am therefore I love me" Astarius Miraculii

"I am in you and you in me, mutual in divine love." William Blake "Love is my gift to the world. I fill myself with love, and I send that love out into the world. How others treat me is their path; how I react is mine." Dr. Wayne Dyer

"Be kind today....to yourself, remember to be a good friend to yourself, accept that you're doing your best, love your perfect imperfections, be mindful of what you need and give it to yourself, and surround yourself with people who honor, love and cherish you for who you are." Lan Lawton

"If you love yourself, you love others. If you hate yourself, you hate others. In relationships with others, it is only you, mirrored." Osho

"I love myself, me being you, you being me, me being us, and us being we, we being love and love being free" Austin Seay

"The ultimate Goal is to feel Unified and Whole Filling up on Love, where there once was a Hole The Gracious Integration of Body, Mind and Soul" Philo Flows

"Hard work is not the path to Well Being. Feeling good is the path to Well-Being. You don't create through action; you create through vibration. And then, your vibration calls action from you." Abraham Hicks"

"The physicists are coming to the same conclusion that the mystics had--that it is just the Vibration from which everything came into being." Dr. Pillai

"Happiness is your nature, it is not wrong to desire it what is wrong is seeking it from outside when it is inside" Ramana Maharshi

"When we awaken to our truth and our purpose in life, we open up a space to be in service and authentically contribute to humanity." "Once we become aware and then make a choice to be the change for others to awaken, we are part of a movement. Simply put, we are generating an abundance of awakening events; we become the generators—the Source—of a movement." Jo Englesson

"Without a visceral connection to our deepest purpose it is difficult to sustain conscious choices, one must receive, ask for guidance and pray for their vision if they don't have one... and once that soul vision comes... one must commit to it; from there the universe will conspire to support your greatest alignment with this vision, with your soul's north star." Aloka

Afterword

"Beautiful soul co creating with me I thank you for the deeds you have done, the deeds you will do. You are the light when I am the dark, a fire sharing their flame with me. Know that I am thankful for you. The amazing potential you are, what a surprise it will be for you to soon see the next level of your awakening. It comes in waves, not all is given at once. You go through life thinking so much, The true task is to be thoughtless and allow it all to come Beautiful soul, how I wish you could see through the eyes of mine knowing who you really are in this grand scene of acting in the drama we call life. What a beautiful time will be had once you have seen the time we have put in this co created world, choosing to go through all of this, because for us it is fun, little do you know that we have done this all together many many times before choosing to forget the memories of our past loves together. Beautiful soul, know that once you remember who you are you will look into that bodies eyes and know and thank them for assisting you in your journey. Giving those gentle pushes through out your life, in different bodies but from the same class room of souls. We know each other so well but it is funny because if I truly told you who you were to me it would ruin the surprise. So we keep co creating together pretending to find each others true love but over and over we find one another and that beautiful in on itself is love." "Remember who you are. Your existence here is but a blink of an eye. This illusion, Although persistent, is just that, an illusion. There is no evil. There is no good. There is just you, not your chemical body, but you your consciousness, your mind. Everything and Everyone, it's just you. Made by you, for you. You are the creator, the only creator and you can do no wrong. So bask in your Holiness, for you are immortal. Your chemical vessel, that thing you call a body may and will die. But you are immortal, eternal. So do as thine will by the whole of the law. The law of one, that you are everything that has or will ever be, And there will be no judgment for your deeds, except that which you give your self. Serve your self or serve your other self, it is always your choice for you are god, and I love you, always have and always will."

By *David Andrew Rodriguez Aka TheWaterMagister.com*

The Light Beings Vision For Humanity

We shall witness a world where civilization is unified in recognition of the truth. A world where we understand our connection to all things and behave with harmonious integrity. Where in that integrity we function in open, honest expression and are both encouraged and supported to do so at all times. We understand how we show up for one another and take ownership and responsibility of our lives in honor of that service. Where unconditional, absolute love is the conquering force and acceptance of all is the guiding principle acknowledging everyone's right to exist. We shall witness a world where we allow ourselves to feel everything with no fear and have command of our emotions as we recognize their role in our own creative abilities. Where creativity is an essential necessity in our way of life. Imagination is cultivated, recognized as a vital asset to our basic human development. We shall witness a civilization that owns its power by living in the strength of its own vulnerability, knowing all aspects of ourselves are valid to our own experiential self. All basic necessities are met and the prosperity of the collective is reflected in our society as what is of the highest good for the people and the environment is always the top priority. All challenges are faced with clarity, understanding, and gratitude as we understand the purpose and function of all experience. We shall witness complete sustainable living, a more harmoniously serving economy, a path greater developed in self-sufficiency with an instinctive order to provide for the all. This includes an education system that evolves as our collective consciousness does and places stock in a student's knowledge of self being just as important to their development as any core curriculum. State of mind is a focal point and the ability to enhance self-awareness is a mandate toward the mastery of our creative powers and our emotional output into the field. Where living in pure awareness sees rigidity give way to the freedom of undeniable growth, shifting through the constant evolution of our conscious thought and ever expanding creative nature. We shall witness a world where we bask in our oneness, elevate our frequency, explore our unlimited creative potential, and deliberately create the reality of our choosing. We shall change, forever and always, what it means to have the human experience.

TRUTH. LOVE. FREEDOM.

THE LIGHT BEINGS COMMUNITY PRINCIPLES

1. KNOW THY SELF
2. OWN THY POWER
3. LIVE FROM THE HEART
4. HONOR THE CONNECTION
5. LIVE INTENTIONALLY
6. LISTEN TO THE BODY
7. FOLLOW THE INTUITION
8. TAKE OWNERSHIP AND RESPONSIBILITY
9. INTERNAL CAUSE, EXTERNAL EFFECT
10. BE DRIVEN BY UNCONDITIONAL LOVE

The Light Beings Community Principles are the embodiment of our way of life and the guidelines in which we live by, according to our foundation and practice. Each principle lives in conscious accordance within themselves and the structure of existence.

THE FACTS

* THE SELF IS LIMITATIONS, BOUNDLESS, AND ALWAYS CONNECTED
* I CREATE MY OWN REALITY FROM WITHIN
* I AM MADE FROM UNCONDITIONAL, ABSOLUTE LOVE
* I EXIST (THEREFORE I MATTER)

* THE SOURCE, THE ALL, IS THE SOURCE OF ALL
  (I AM ALWAYS CONNECTED TO SOURCE)
* THE TRUTH IS EFFORTLESS AND UNCOMPROMISING
* MY POWER IS IN THE PRESENT (ONLY THE PRESENT EXISTS)

What is *The Light Beings Community*?

The Light Beings Community is a communal society united in the choice to live in uncompromising truth, to thrive in unconditional love, and to expand the boundaries of our unlimited creative potential as a collective. In this united resonance we offer motivation, support, encouragement, guidance, and accountability along the path of greater self realization.

What does it mean to be a *Light Being*?

A *Light Being* is someone who can witness every aspect of themselves and embrace it all in the love that they are, becoming a guiding space of awareness and inspiration for remembering truth.

About the Author

Namaste, I'm from a very small town in Pennsylvania known as Farrell. Growing up, I was raised very well by a single loving mother and a loving father whom did his best to be there for me. My mother made a living working as a cook making minimum wage and still managed to somehow provide food, clothes and shelter for my sisters and I. As a child we lived paycheck to paycheck. Seeing my mother struggle and being an independent minded child, I soon found myself at the age of nine getting a paper route to be able to give mom less stress while gaining money management skills. Growing up into my teenage years I maintained that same mentality, doing what I could, mainly selling marijuana to relieve my mother from stress of having to provide me with anything more than food and shelter.

My senior year of high school I was a middle linebacker and captain of the defense with dreams of being recruited by a D-I university then going to the NFL. Towards the end of the season I took a helmet to the knee and tore my acl and mcl. Being injured I was unable to play in the playoffs where most recruits find there players, which meant I did not get a scholarship to a D-I School. I am very grateful now for the experience because I would not be the man I am today if it hadn't taken place exactly as it did.

In the summer of 2006, after finishing my freshman year of college. I was introduced to my soul brother David, after a few weeks of being friends he offered me a DVD pertaining documentaries. I did not know that the DVD was going to be a pivotal point in my life at the time. After watching the DVD, a light switch turned on in my head and suddenly It felt like I was awakened from a hypnotic trance. Which is why I give so much gratitude to the guy who took my knee out because if not I would have never went to Clarion to meet David. Now awakened from the trance, I began educating myself and those around me. Doing thorough research upon many subjects, I soon realized there were a lot of things going on in the world and within myself I was unaware of.

Still wondering what to do in life, I soon began to seek guidance from within. It didn't take long for me to realize my purpose in life. My purpose on Earth is to make a difference today for the youth of tomorrow. The question then came, how? My answer ~ Promote and spread the message of peace, love and unity and to be a source of inspiration to all. While expressing what many have continuously noted in the past and yet it has become a lost art; Know thyself, unconditionally love thyself, thy neighbor and thy enemy as thy self.

In the winter of 2006, I felt it was necessary to leave school to pursue my purpose. I knew I could reach more people outside of the small town of Clarion. Within a couple days of contemplating, I left Clarion with a 3.2 GPA that winter on my own behalf trusting I was making the correct decision. Though I left the university, I continued to attend the school of life. Being home with little to do, I began studying and reading on a daily bases upon many subjects with no judgment or discrimination with a complete open and clear mind. I also began to put together compilations of documenatries with various informative documentaries, giving people an opportunity to have a resource to educate and empower themselves and others. I began to distribute them free to the people in my community on a small scale, doing my part to make a difference.

Being home from school, I wondered what could I do to contribute and make more of a difference. I decided to volunteer with an old coach of mine, with the opportunity to be able to share some of my experiences and wisdom with the children. After my last season coaching football,

I applied for a position in Pittsburgh working with youth which required a bachelors degree. Thankfully, I was given the position do to my experience of coaching and working with children. I soon moved to Pittsburgh to accept the position. The position entailed working in parks, cleaning, building, maintaining trails and teaching environmental education while having the opportunity to mentor and share wisdom as well. After working with the student conservation association for two years I chose to utilize my last paycheck to start my own vending business on the campus of the university of Pittsburgh. I chose to call it T-RAVS BBQ LAB. The business began to grow quickly, and before you knew it, T-RAV'S became the place to be on Pitt campus. Subsequently, I became a vegetarian not long after being intuitively guided to stop eating what was no longer serving me and begin to expand my energy, so chose to eat energy 'fruits and vegetables because I am what I eat. Despite my lifestyle change, I chose to run the business for three more years due to the love and loyalty of my customers. The business wasn't reflecting my moral standards at all. Having studied holistic healing, knowing whats good for the body and whats not, I chose to listen to my heart and decided to shut down the business because it conflicted with my spiritual aspirations and ultimately was distracting me from my purpose. I know my purpose for coming here to this planet wasn't to serve flesh to the people on a platter. Knowing I am here for something bigger than myself and any amount of money.

In the summer of 2012 after being reminded I am a minister, I decided to answer the calling to become a non denominational traveling minister with faith source would provide. I soon began to pursue my purpose in life. Spreading the message of inner peace, self love and oneness with the hope of removing all man made divisions that divide the people of the world. So we can all truly live in unity without the burden of judgments and prejudice. To hopefully make a difference today for the children of tomorrow.

Soon After shutting down the business I decided to sell everything I owned, everything but the assets I've obtained to serve the mission. I heard a calling to go to Jamaica. Knowing not one native of Jamaica, I decided to go to Jamaica with hopes to have the opportunity to learn and make a difference somehow. Also with the hopes of possibly finding my roots and maybe meet some family. I also wanted to take time to find myself through a lot of meditation, reading, and writing in the rain forest. While in Jamaica I chose to make a difference by speaking to the people and handed out dvd's pertaining various subjects such as self empowerment, self sustainability and holistic healing modalities while giving love and appreciation to everyone I came in contact with.

While in Jamaica I found my roots after going to the registrar building giving them my great, great, great, great grandfathers name, three hours of research later, I found my ancestor and I also met some family as well after appearing on a radio show that assist people with finding family. I was also blessed with the accommodation of many Jamaicans that gave me great hospitality, which gave me the opportunity to meditate, read, and write while having the honor to socialize with many Jamaican natives. Overall the experience was great, I can say I accomplished everything I went to do and much more, I even found out I can sing while in the forest. I know I have unfinished business and plan to go back to continue the mission.

After returning from Jamaica I returned to Pittsburgh, then shortly after I heard the calling to go to Peru to learn the ways of plant medicine to bring the knowledge back to the states. I decided to stay in Peru for a little over forty days. For half of the time I was there I spent it with a friend I met from Peru and his family in Ica and Lima. Then spent the remainder of my time in the amazon jungle learning from various currandero's or thought of as shamans in the states. While in the jungle I had the opportunity to not only partake with the sacred plant medicine auayahuasca, I was also blessed with the opportunity to cook and prepare it as well. While in the jungle I met a brother by the name of drum bum and the sun, He wrote over three chapbooks which sparked some inspiration in me to compile all my poems and create this book you are reading here today.

Being a child that has grown up in America in the 20th century, witnessing many different presidents come and go. I have seen reasonable spiritual and intellectual progress in today's society. Today it's time time maximize and take action and begin to be the change I would like to see, unifying together to create solutions to the problems that we all see on a day to day basis. No longer depending on others to change things for us. Growing up in America as a multiracial child, I have experienced masses amounts of discrimination from all sides of the spectrum, from African, Caucasian, Asian etc and from the rich and even the less fortunate. I have been given these blessings of experiences that ultimately molded me into the person I am today. I give thanks to have been given those experiences to now love myself fully and have a vision and solutions to today's most important issues. I have an opportunity to unite and eliminate the inherited social virus of racism, classism and religious differences that have been handed down generation to generation. By simply choosing to hand down another virus to go viral of unconditional love, not just for the the sake of my mother, father, nieces, nephews, sisters and brothers, but for everyone and all future generations to come.

Now is the time to see all the barriers, judgments and beliefs in my life, time to reflect and see if there are any old stories of limitation hindering my growth and expansion. Now is the time to see that it is ok to open my heart again, it is ok to be vulnerable and transparent. Now is the time to allow my experiences and wisdom gained in my life to be the guiding light for those around me. Now is the time to expand my love where there may have been conditions or judgments and learn that I am everything and simply by loving all versions of myself I am choosing to love everything. Now is the time to allow love in again, if I may have closed off my heart due to a past experience. It is ok to trust again and remember all of my experiences happened in divine time in service to the development my being. Now is the time to see there is nothing out to get me and I am safe. Remembering I create my reality and everything in it, taking ownership and responsibility of everything arising. Now is the time to recognize our similarities, and take into consideration that quantum physics proves that everything is 99.9999% space. Now is the time have respect and compassion for each of our unique differences as well. Now seeing that together all of our unique puzzle pieces create a puzzle that is able to rise above any situation life brings us. Now is the time to reconnect to nature. Seeing the beauty of the flower buds, songs of the birds and wisdom of the trees. Now is the time to connect to my intuition within, the divine spark residing within everyone of us. Taking time to meditate to hear my guidance showing me the way by tuning in and listening to the heart beyond the rational mind.

With love and gratitude,
Travis 'Natural' Huntley

Contact the author at:
For Spoken Word and Musical Performance, Hosting festivals and events, Wedding Ceremony, Empowerment Workshops, Keynote Inspirational Speaking, 1on1 Intuitive Guidance, Youth and Adult Mindfulness Coaching, Reiki, Heart Thread, Energy/Bodywork, Vegan Cooking/ Health Coaching, Transformational Coaching

Naturalivity.net
Naturallivity101@gmail.com
Facebook.com/yourdivineallthetime

Peace Love Unity

The peace love and unity foundation is a platform with cumulative resources that offers the people freedom to choose a more harmonious and empowered way of life, with greater knowledge of self and the ability to love at a greater capacity. The mission is to utilize art in various forms such as poems, stickers, clothing and murals to empower and unite the people. Uniting all citizens so we as a whole can come together and make decisions, no longer depending on the state to make decisions for us. We travel the country utilizing, empowering pamphlets, stickers, art and speaking opportunities. We also reach out to the artists, actors, athletes, celebrities and others of influence to utilize all platforms such as public appearances, social media and main stream media to influence and empower the people, raising awareness to unify and love each other unconditionally.

Contact:
www.Facebook.com/PeaceLuvUnity
PeaceLuvUnity1@gmail.com
Peace Love Unity
Peace-Love-Unity.Org

Acknowledgments

I give gratitude to my family, tribe, angels, ancestors and guides for your support and guidance. I give thanks to all whom assisted in the creation of this book. I'd also like to give thanks to everyone who came into my life in some way or another. I give gratitude to source for the opportunity to experience a life on Earth. I give gratitude to those reading this book for showing up here on Earth in this now moment. I acknowledge you as myself expressing in another form. I give love to you and to all in all time, space and dimensions